Our Ballet Class

By STEPHANIE RIVA SORINE

Photographs by DANIEL S. SORINE

Alfred A. Knopf · New York

Acknowledgments

Thanks to the editorial, design, and production people who have treated us and our book so well.

Special thanks to Cordelia Newlin, Jannette Hitz, Claude Kaplan, Gabrielle Liberatore, Elissa McLean, and their parents.

We appreciate the cooperation of Gail Kachadurian and Sherrie Hinkle at The Dance Movement school in New York City.

And we are especially grateful to Stephanie's mother, Shirley Bassoff Silverman, for having brought Stephanie to ballet class so many years ago.

This is a Borzoi Book published by Alfred A. Knopf, Inc.

Published in the United States by Alfred A. Knopf, Inc.,
New York, and simultaneously in Canada by Random House of Canada Limited, Toronto.
Distributed by Random House, Inc., New York.

Library of Congress Cataloging in Publication Data
Sorine, Stephanie Riva. Our ballet class.
Summary: A little girl describes her weekly ballet lesson.
1. Ballet dancing—Juvenile literature. [1. Ballet dancing] I. Sorine, Daniel S. II Title.
GV1787.5.S66 1981 792.8'2 80-28927
ISBN 0-394-85041-6 ISBN 0-394-94821-1 (lib. bdg.)
Manufactured in the United States of America Designed by Mina Greenstein 0 9 8 7 6 5 4 3 2 1

For the parents and guardians
who give children the chance
to experience ballet

OUR BALLET CLASS

I'm Cordelia. I go to ballet class once a week.

Jannette, Gabrielle, Elissa, and Claude are in the class too.

Our teacher is a real dancer. She wears toe shoes, and a ballet skirt over her leotard.

First we work at the barre. "Leg up, leg down—now *stretch!*" our teacher tells us. The steps don't seem like real dancing, but she says they will make us strong and flexible.

She says all ballet dancers, even the most famous ones, begin their classes this way.

We do a lot of bending: forward . . .

backward . . .

sideways.

When we bend forward, we try to touch our heads to our knees.

Nobody can do that yet. Our teacher says that if we work hard, we'll be able to someday.

Our teacher is nice. When I do something wrong, she corrects me without yelling. When I do it right, she says, “Cordelia, that’s very good!”

Most of the time I behave.

But sometimes I like to fool around.

So do Jannette and Gabrielle.

Then the teacher gets mad and says, "Must I teach you girls a new step, called punishment?"

After that I try hard to pay attention. I want to do the steps like a dancer.

Jannette does them really well.

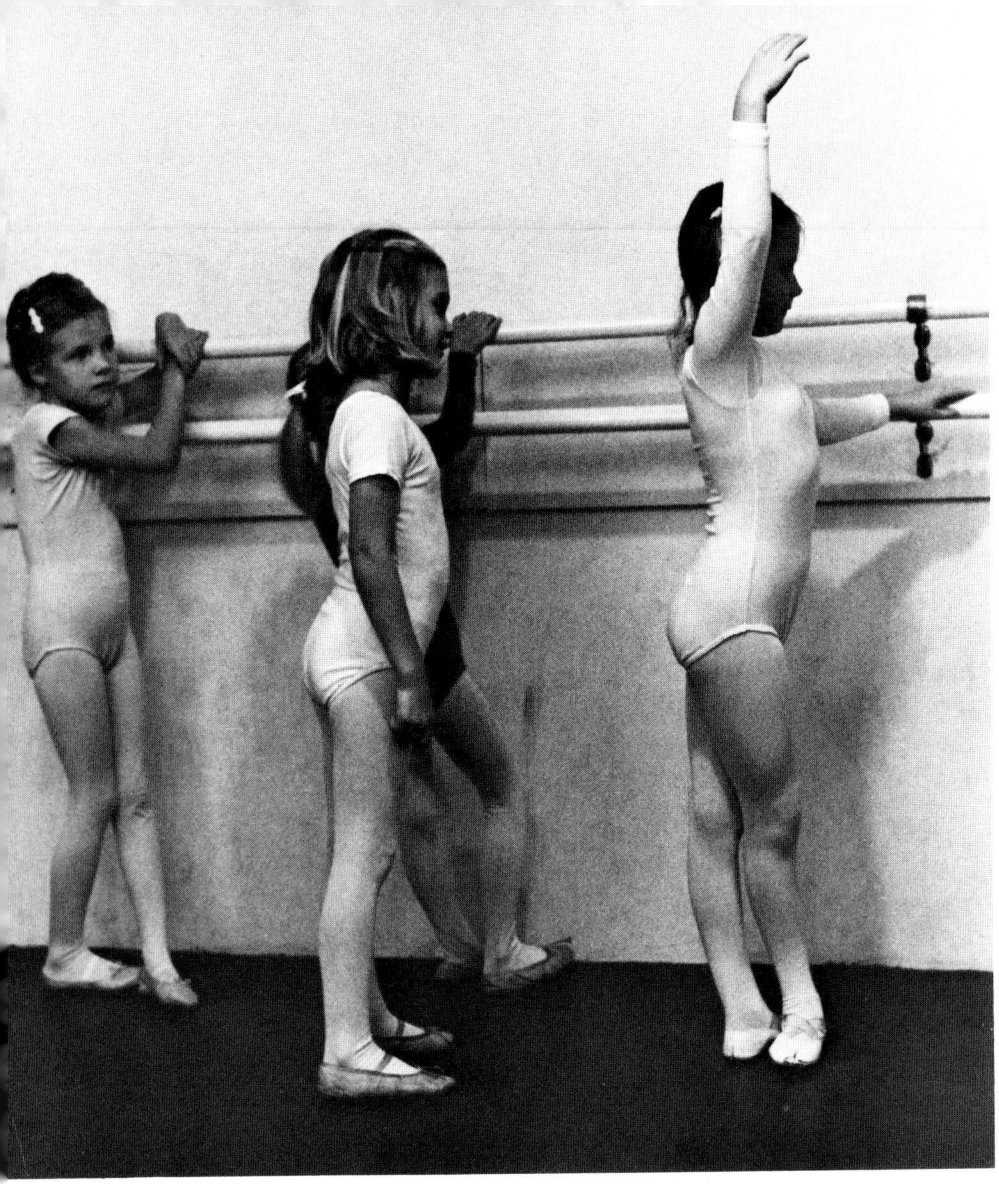

Sometimes our teacher says, “Girls, watch how Jannette does it.”

And sometimes Jannette helps by showing me what I’m doing wrong.

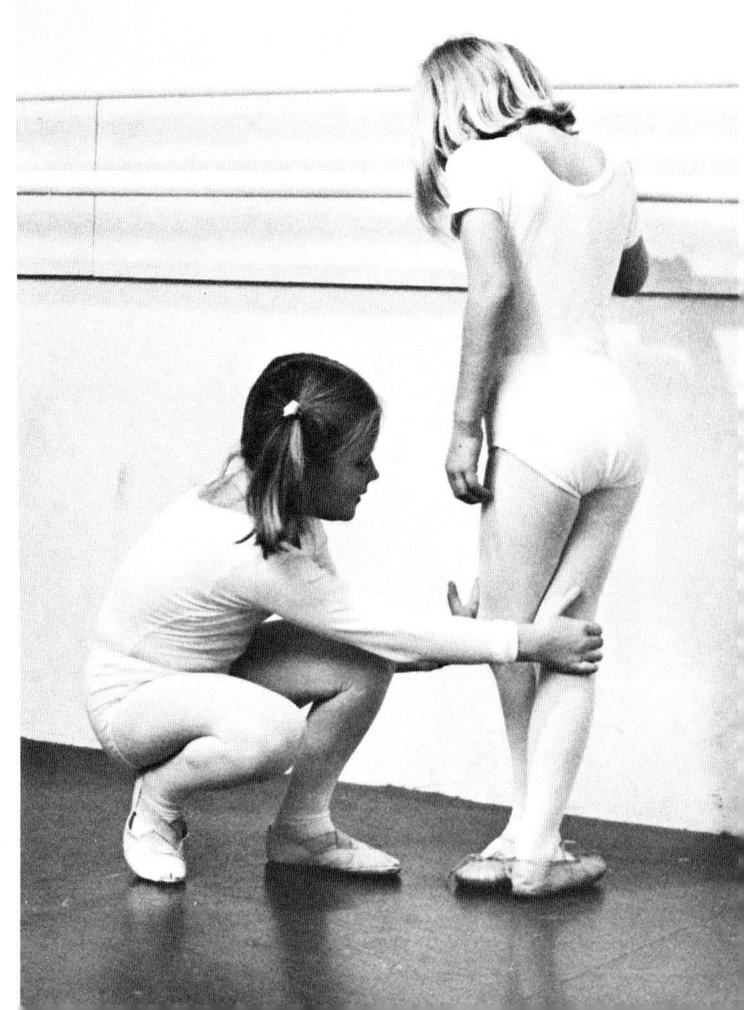

"Cordelia, can you do this?" she says. I try, but it's hard to hold my leg straight and point my foot at the same time.

The more I practice, though, the easier it gets.

When the teacher shows us a new step, I always think, "That looks so hard—I could never do it."

But then she says, "Who wants to try this step?"
"I do! I do!" we all shout.

Maybe the barre is too high, or maybe I'm too short—
but I still try everything.

"It's time to stretch," says the teacher. "Sit as tall as you can, and make your back nice and straight."

It looks easy when she does it, but it's not. "Come on, muscles—stretch!" I say.

Jannette can't touch her toes, but I can touch mine. . . .

Claude is like a rubber band. Nobody can do the splits as well as she can.

When I do a backbend, the floor turns into the ceiling, and I get dizzy, so the teacher holds me steady.

Jannette can do
backbends alone.
"She looks like a
bridge," I tell Gabrielle.
"Okay, let's be
boats," she says.

But then Jannette starts
to laugh, and the bridge
falls down.

The best part of ballet class is when our teacher says,
"All right, girls, you may put on your costumes."

Dancing in a tutu makes me feel like a real ballerina!
Everyone’s tutu is different.

We count ruffles to see
who has the most.

The teacher puts on the music for our dance called "Flowers." "Line up behind Cordelia," she says.

I like to be first.
I try extra hard to
remember the steps
and do them
correctly.

"Listen to the music,
follow the counts,"
says our teacher.

My arms are petals . . .

moved by the wind . . .

reaching for the sun.

“That’s becoming
very beautiful,”
says the teacher.
She sounds pleased.

At the end we get the giggles....

But we have to straighten up and take our bow, because our ballet class is almost over. We can hear the next class talking in the hallway.

We curtsy to the teacher. . .

and kiss her goodbye.

"See you next week!"

STEPHANIE RIVA SORINE began dancing at the age of three. She trained at the School of American Ballet and at the Royal Ballet School in London, apprenticed with the Harkness Ballet, and danced as a soloist with the Austrian ballet. She teaches classes in ballet and dance movement to children and adults in New York City.

DANIEL S. SORINE was born in Paris, France, and raised in Monaco. He attended Le Rosey and Institut Florimont in Switzerland and the Lycée Français de New York. His photographs have appeared in *Life, Time, Newsweek, People, The New York Times, Dancemagazine,* and other publications in America and abroad.

The Sorines, who now live in New York City, have been married since 1977. Their previous collaborations include two books for young readers, *Imagine That! It's Modern Dance* and *At Every Turn! It's Ballet*; the acclaimed adult book *Dancershoes*; and Ballantine's ballet calendars.